Australian Animals
Koalas

By Sara Louise Kras

Consulting Editor: Gail Saunders-Smith, PhD

Content Consultant: Bob Cleaver, owner
Wombat Rise Sanctuary, a home for rescued Australian wildlife
Sandleton, South Australia

Capstone
press®

Mankato, Minnesota

Pebble Plus is published by Capstone Press,
151 Good Counsel Drive, P.O. Box 669, Mankato, Minnesota 56002.
www.capstonepub.com

Library of Congress Cataloging-in-Publication Data
Kras, Sara Louise
    Koalas / by Sara Louise Kras.
    p. cm. — (Pebble plus. Australian animals)
    Includes bibliographical references and index.
    Summary: "Simple text and photographs present koalas, how they look,
where they live, and what they do" — Provided by publisher.
    ISBN-13: 978-1-4296-3310-9 (library binding)
    ISBN-13: 978-1-4296-3868-5 (pbk.)
    1. Koala — Juvenile literature. I. Title. II. Series.
QL737.M384K73 2010
599.2'5 — dc22   2008052561

Editorial Credits
Jenny Marks, editor; Bobbie Nuytten and Ted Williams, designers; Svetlana Zhurkin, media researcher

Photo Credits
Ardea/D. Parer & E. Parer-Cook, 15
Creatas, 13
iStockphoto/Amanda Rohde, 19
Shutterstock/aliciahh, 17; Ian Scott, 11; Kaspars Grinvalds, 5; Kitch Bain, 21; Mark Higgins, 9; Susan Flashman, 7;
    Tijmen, cover, 1

Note to Parents and Teachers

The Australian Animals set supports national science standards related to life science. This book
describes and illustrates koalas. The images support early readers in understanding the text. The
repetition of words and phrases helps early readers learn new words. This book also introduces
early readers to subject-specific vocabulary words, which are defined in the Glossary section.
Early readers may need assistance to read some words and to use the Table of Contents,
Glossary, Read More, Internet Sites, and Index sections of the book.

Printed in the United States of America in North Mankato, Minnesota.
072011
6321VMI

Table of Contents

Living in Australia 4

Eating and Drinking 10

Growing Joeys 14

Staying Safe 18

Glossary 22

Read More 23

Internet Sites 23

Index 24

Living in Australia

What is that gray, fuzzy animal
sleeping on a branch?
It is a marsupial from Australia
called a koala.

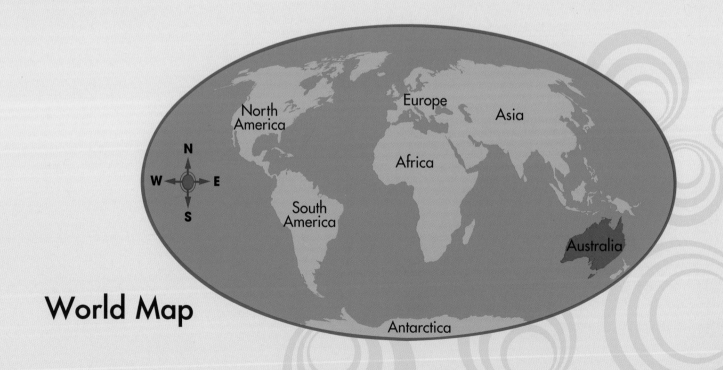

World Map

Koalas live only in Australia.

They spend most of their lives

in eucalyptus trees.

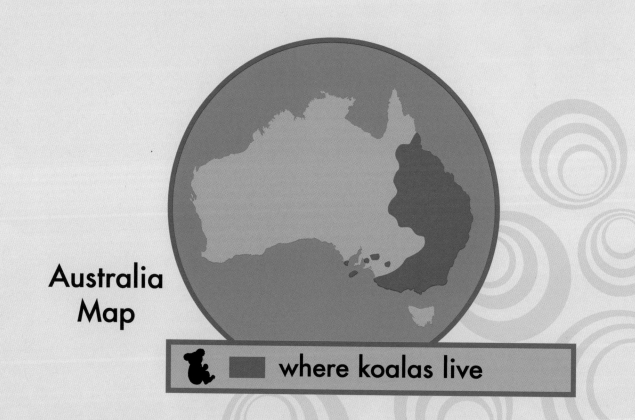

Australia
Map

where koalas live

Strong arms and legs

help koalas climb.

They have two thumbs

and sharp claws

to hold on tight.

Eating and Drinking

At night koalas munch

on eucalyptus leaves.

Their wide noses

smell the best leaves to eat.

Koalas don't leave the trees
to get a drink.
They get water from eating
lots of juicy leaves.

Growing Joeys

Baby koalas are called joeys. For six months, a newborn joey stays in its mother's pouch. Newborn koalas are the size of a jelly bean.

Koalas teach their joeys
how to climb and find food.
After one year, young koalas
can live on their own.

Staying Safe

Koalas' biggest danger is people.
People cut down eucalyptus trees
to use the land and the wood.
Cars can hit koalas.

Land has been set aside
for koalas in reserves.
Koalas living on reserves
are protected and safe.

Glossary

eucalyptus — a tall evergreen tree with a strong scent; koalas eat eucalyptus leaves.

joey — a young koala

marsupial — an animal that carries its young in a pouch

pouch — a pocket-like flap of skin

protected — kept safe from danger

reserve — land that is protected so that animals may live there safely

Read More

Arnold, Caroline. *A Koala's World.* Caroline Arnold's Animals. Minneapolis: Picture Window Books, 2008.

Bodden, Valerie. *Koalas.* Amazing Animals. Mankato, Minn.: Creative Education, 2009.

Eckart, Edana. *Koala.* Animals of the World. New York: Children's Press, 2005.

Internet Sites

FactHound offers a safe, fun way to find Internet sites related to this book. All of the sites on FactHound have been researched by our staff.

Here's all you do:

Visit *www.facthound.com*

FactHound will fetch the best sites for you!

Index

arms, 8

Australia, 4, 6

claws, 8

climbing, 8

danger, 18

drinking, 12

eating, 10, 12

eucalyptus trees, 6, 18

joeys, 14, 16

leaves, 10, 12

marsupials, 4

noses, 10

pouches, 14

reserves, 20

sleeping, 4

smelling, 10

thumbs, 8

water, 12

Word Count: 166
Grade: 1
Early-Intervention Level: 24